written and illustrated
by Christine Davis

# Forever Paws

Printed in China

Lighthearted Press Inc.
P.O. Box 90125
Portland, OR 97290
www.lightheartedpress.com

ISBN-13: 978-0-9659225-5-5
ISBN-10: 0-9659225-5-3

10 9 8 7 6 5

From the author...

"You know," someone told me once, "you've never really written a book about coping with the loss of an animal companion."

While that was true, I thought I'd said everything I was meant to say about loss in my books *For Every Dog An Angel* and *For Every Cat An Angel*. Then I unexpectedly lost my beloved cat, Dickens, followed a few months later by my forever cat, Pippen...and my world fell apart.

*Remember what you are feeling – there's another book to be written.*

I heard those words over and over again. They came in whispers on the wind. They spilled like sparkling droplets into my tears. It became crystal clear to me that the loss of my dear cats was a loving gift from my precious feline friends...a sort of cosmic "thump on the head" to keep me on my path!

I offer this little book for anyone who is missing a much-loved animal companion. I hope you will be uplifted by the vibrant colors and joyful critters – that's what Dickens and Pippen showed me! On those days when you're feeling lost and the tears won't end, remember a gift has been left on your heart that will one day light your way back to the four-legged friend who loves you.

With love and gratitude,
Chris Davis

For all the

critters

who have left

their

paw prints

in

our hearts

THE WONDROUS GIFT OF FOREVER PAWS

$W$henever a puppy or kitten
is born on earth it is given
a wondrous gift – the gift
of forever paws.

"Remember," the young one is told, "your glowing paws celebrate the shining spirit within you, but only you can see their brilliance. They will take you on grand adventures, and lead you to new friends, but their true purpose is to guide you to the person who would welcome you home.

Should you find
the one who is meant to
hold your gentle heart,
the gift of the paws
will keep you connected
always and forever."

So dogs and cats come into our world, and one by one they find us. They weave themselves into our lives like furry tapestries and blanket us with their love.

All too soon, there comes a day when our animal companions must continue on their journey without us. So they step lightly from their old and hurting bodies, and ready their paws to carry them to the bridge that will take them onward.

Just before they leave this world, every animal you loved on earth takes a little piece of your heart, which they carry on a ribbon that floats in the sky.

In its place, they leave on your heart a print from a brilliant forever paw, a gift that will one day light your way back to the four-legged friend who loves you.

Dogs and cats may also bring along a favorite toy or trinket on their journey, which explains why some people find a much-loved plaything is suddenly missing!

Then it's off to the bridge in the stars, where angel pets watch over earthly friends and wait for their loved ones to join them.

nimal companions know how hard it is for you to say goodbye to them. They see every tear that is cried whenever a treasured pet is lost. All of these tears flow like a river out of this world and into the next.

Each evening, just at sunset,
the animals gather at the bridge to drink
from the river of tears, for all of the
sadness has been left behind and
only the love remains.

When a person carries a forever paw print,
they can never be separated from the animal
who left it on their heart.

Should you wish you could be a tall tree,
with arms so long you could reach your
furry angel, never forget your beloved pet is
peacefully sleeping in your branches.

If you wish the Big Dipper would lift you up
     to the one whose paw prints dance in your heart,
try searching the sky for a bouquet of stars
          sent with love from your critter above.

Furry friends love to visit when you are sleeping.
If you dream that your dog is chatting
with a flamingo, or your cat is purring
contentedly in the arms of a frog,
it probably is!

And if whispers come in the night, telling of other creatures in need of a loving home, remember the heart of an animal lover can hold many paw prints.

The E-Collar Choir

In time, you will come to know that your angel pet is doing well, happy to be young and renewed. You may even see your critter in far off heavenly fields, playing with other angel friends.

WOOFS 'N PURRS

Take Out

Ask About Today's Special
Ice Cream    Sardines
Pockets without pills
        Cheese    Biscuits
Che  Treat   Tuna Fish

One day, when your time on the earth has ended, the paw prints that you hold in your heart will light your way to the bridge in the stars. All your animal friends will be there to welcome you home with woofs and purrs.

WHEN A PAW PRINT FINDS

A FOREVER HEART NOTHING WILL EVER KEEP THEM APART

Then you will
cross the bridge together, paw print and heart
forever entwined, never...ever...to be parted again.

We hope you enjoyed this
Lighthearted Press book. To order additional copies,
please call our toll free order number 1-877-385-6837
or visit us online at www.lightheartedpress.com.


Books by Christine Davis:

Forever Paws
For Every Dog An Angel
For Every Cat An Angel
The Shelter Dog
Old Dog and the Christmas Wish


Lighthearted Press Inc.
P.O. Box 90125 * Portland, Oregon 97290
503-786-3085 (Phone)
503-786-0315 (Fax)
1-877-385-6837 (Toll free)
www.lightheartedpress.com